DiaMind

A Mindful Journey to Your Essence

DiaMind

Preliminary Remark and Disclaimer:

This book addresses mentally stable people with a desire for personal growth and wisdom. It is written for people, who feel emotionally and mentally confident and are able to cope with potential inner feelings of insecurity. It is highly important to seek professional support by a life coach or a therapist if necessary.

This book in no shape or form replaces counseling by a doctor or a therapist and the author disclaims all liability.

The statements made in the book refer to Germany in 2020.

Be the Change

You

Want to See in The

World.

Mahatma Gandhi

Dear reader,

I wrote this book for you.

I gather herein all the wisdom and insights from the bottom of my soul, which I gained from my experience, and all wisdom I discovered through readings. My aim was to present this in a clear, hopefully easily approachable manner. On top of being instructional, I hope that this book is also fun to read.

In each section you have space for personal reflection focusing on the topic discussed therein. I invite you - just for the sake of your own development and growth - to answer the questions honestly and also note impulses and thoughts. Following this path, you have the chance to gain a little more enlightenment with each chapter.

My desire is that you experience joy while growing and finding the trail to your potential and your inner diamond!

The journey is the destination and this journey is amazing!

Yours faithfully,

Lea-Johanna

Introduction "Why DiaMind?"

The Journey Of A Butterfly

Past

1. Self-awareness
2. Projections
3. Mental Injuries
4. Entidentification – Releasing The Fixation
5. Programming, Imprints and Beliefs
6. Childhood And Inner Child
7. Parents
8. Promising And Forgiving – The End of The 'Drama-Game'

Present

9. Consciousness – Or: Being Aware
10. Inspiration
11. Energy Follows Attention
12. Motions Of Thinking
13. Responsibility
14. Decisions And Intuition
15. Emotional Eating
16. Alone Or: All-One
17. The World And I

Future

18. Who Am I And Who Will I Be?

19. (R)Evolutionary Partnership

20. Potential Evolvement

21. My Vision – Or: Wishes Are Memories That Come From The Future

22. Personal Growth– Or: Towards The Sun

23. Last But Not Least: Everything Is A Process

24. My Personal Insights Of The Mindful Journey To My Essence

Enlightening Reading For Further Study

Introduction "**Why DiaMind?**"

'DiaMind' to me stands for two sides of a medal. In my experience, it is possible to discover positivity in every situation, in every person and in every negative experience by gaining self-knowledge through personal reflection. This happens once you flip the medal from the dark to the bright side. This process has the power to shift your own reality in a wonderful way!

The word 'mind' stands for intellect and rationality, yet it also includes a spiritual dimension. For some years now, the scientific field of brain research has focused on the neuroplasticity of the brain. Contrary to early assumptions, our brain is not completely finished once we are adults. Our brains rather develop and transform throughout our entire life. Considering this, ways of thinking especially new ones, new thoughts, feelings and interpretations have the power to change our perception. This leads to a noticeable re-experience and new awareness about what we think our reality is.

Deep down inside of the "DiaMind" your very individual diamond is hidden. I invite you to discover your own diamond while travelling to your essence with the help of this book.

However, before your very own personal journey to your essence begins, I would like share my story with you. This is very dear to me, as I have not always felt so clear and calm, full of joy and courage as I do in my life at the moment. I would like to show you that this book is not just made of theory and philosophy but at the same time consists of practice, which has been personally experienced. Feel free to skip my story altogether or come back to it at your leisure and start with your own journey straight away! This book is structured in a systematic manner from the past via the present to the future and it is recommended you follow this path. However, it is **your** decision whether you work your way through the book in order or begin with those chapters which are particularly interesting to you. All topics are linked to each other yet at the same time they are self-contained.

Enjoy your journey!

Lea-Johanna

<u>The Journey Of A Butterfly</u>

About ten years ago, I experienced the lowest point of my life. My first child was 2.5 years and we lived separated from its father. I was so far removed from myself and any joy in living that even now I struggle to describe it. At the time, the separation with my child from my partner was the most drastic thing that had happened to me and the thing that had scared me the most.

Looking back on this time, it was the greatest challenge that I could possibly have encountered in my life. Similarly, to my studies in philosophy, this challenge opened up an enormous space for personal development and inner growth. I started to travel inside of me, to get to know and liberate myself. At the beginning, I felt trapped as if I had been inside a cocoon like a caterpillar, disconnected from my life, from other people, from love and, most important, from myself. Everything inside of me was heavy and dark. I could not even imagine that my life would ever be good and full of light again. not in a million years would I have imagined a life, which is so golden and bright as I am able to experience today. In addition to studying philosophy during my time at university, I read a great number of books concerned with self-love, psychology, successful relationships as well as spirituality and personality development. Whenever I was working on an inner issue without being able to solve it by myself, I was seeking the support of friends and professional coaches. To this day, I stand by this approach as development and inner growth are a never-ending process!

Approximately five years after my personal low point, I realized for the first time that I am *really* the creator of my life through my thoughts. Right before my point zero, I had had the strongest fear that a separation from the father of my first child was possible and I, therefore, a single mom. I was constantly focusing on this fear.

So, this is what happened: As I was so entangled by this thought, my whole energy led to this event. Due to that, it *had to manifest*. This is a ‚good' example of the strong potency of our thoughts and the principle that energy follows attention – always. The science of Quantum Physics is able to explain this process in great detail. By leading the attention towards the focused event – no matter whether it is something positive or negative – it becomes bigger as it is constantly 'fed' with energy. In my case: The separation from my partner, father of my first child, materialized.

While dealing with my inner world and the 'cleanup' initiated by the separation, I began to reflect on various aspects of my life: The relationships with my parents and siblings, the meaning of my life, how I would like to shape and experience motherhood and partnership, my thoughts on my personal freedom in particular and about liberty in general, to name just a few. Through the process of those years – a process you are invited to go through yourself in your very own way, supported by this book – I found out that the perception of my life as a cocoon of unfreedom and darkness, in fact, yielded a decisive advantage, a psychological gain for me:

This cocoon was familiar to me and, therefore, offered security. On the one hand, I realized that inner freedom comes at the price of outer security. On the other hand, familiar security takes the toll of unfreedom. I had experienced it as offering me security. However, I still had a choice. This time I decided to choose freedom, cleared up relationships sometimes in a painful way, worked my way through mental pain, deidentified myself from it – and overcame it. Mental pain is likely to accompany processes of self-recognition and clarification, and that is OK. To me mental pains are growing pains like the pain while giving birth: This pain seems sometimes necessary to go through while being in the process of renaissance. The long-term gain of a mental topic processed through transformation, experiencing and finally acceptance is that the issue stops being an issue after what I call: **The mental and emotional rebirth.** If a similar issue returns in the future, it will be on a different level and you will be able to approach it with serenity and a peaceful mind.

I let go of everything that did not belong to me such as certain thoughts, feelings, people, things as well as concepts of life. And I was richly rewarded in return: Giving up security and experiencing this feeling of insecurity was just the first step in this process. The more I grew and developed, the more I gained *real* security within me. The kind of security which only continues growing and which carries me through my life. A security that is above all not an ego-security, which blocks any questioning of what is believed, because otherwise it can be easily shaken. Ego-security has given way to a security of the heart, which is still there even when everything is in question and in a state of change. I feel that this is a rich gift for this process. And it encourages me to continue my way of personal growth, inner development and self-expression.

In my life, the most decisive turning point occurred once I accepted the entire responsibility for myself, let go of me feeling as a victim of my life situation and acknowledged myself as the creator of my life.

After I had developed the *freedom from* within me - the freedom of everything that I no longer chose to experience in my life - life let me enjoy the experience of the *freedom to* (see Erich Fromm: Escape from Freedom). The *freedom to* includes all possibilities I am able to create in my life by choice. This gave me a lot of support for developing a fulfilled life and achieving my goals and dreams. From that moment on, I knew which things I did **not** want experience nor create in my life, for instance the separation I have earlier described. Even though separations at times might be necessary, I would like to approach such an impactful event less like a victim and more as an active party filled with love and confidence. So, I asked myself the following question: What is it, I **want** to experience in my life then?

In 2013, I founded The Practice of Philosophy "freiSein – Praxis für Kommunikation und Philosophie" ("be free – Office for Communication and Philosophy") in Kiel, Northern Germany, and began to support people on their journey into a life of more inner peace and freedom.

Reading large amounts of books concerning partnership and going through a few short relationships myself again taught me many lessons–, some quite painful –, I came to the point where I was *really* willing to be a part of a life partnership seeing eye-to-eye on every level with room for development and personal growth. This was over five years ago, at the beginning of 2015. Today, I am very grateful to experience and grow within a free and connected, - yes, you could say - a (r)evolutionary partnership. My deep desire to have children has been fulfilled in various ways. Today, I am the mother of a colorful, rowdy, happy and evolving patchwork-family with five children.

Every day, I am unspeakable grateful for this rich, golden marriage and multifaced family – due to the potential of growth and despite challenges. Or is it, in fact, because of these manifold challenges and possibilities to grow?

Through all these processes, the philosophical themes of clarity, self-knowledge, connection, responsibility and freedom have emerged as my life themes. In every area of my life, I try to follow these principles, support and empower people in their life in a private context as well as in a professional one. I am and I have always been grinded in the ocean of life like a diamond and I have gained a self-acknowledgement as a philosophical "midwife of life". This refers to the Socratic dialogue method, the maieutic, derived from the midwifery. For me, this feels like a vocation, supporting and empowering people to go through processes of self-reflection, to gain inner freedom and lightness within themselves, to change their perspective and to discover hidden possibilities.

And now?

My current vision has been rising ever more clearly from my soul for years and appears more contoured and clearer in my mind's eye every day. I wish to create a place of consciousness, of growing and becoming for other people. A holy place for healing, perhaps by the sea, which gives the soul - in the sense of a **soul protection area** (according to Eugen Roth, German poet) - space, time and opportunities to feel, unfold and be. A joy garden and the sea invite you to pause in nature, they give you inspiration and connection with everything that is. Above all, this place allows you to hear your own inner voice (again) and to gain new insights about yourself and the world.

***

Past

1. Self-Awareness

This book is all about self-awareness and self-knowledge. In order to grow and develop, it is necessary to be honest with yourself. Even if it hurts and it means that you have to leave your loved and cozy comfort zone. "Recognize yourself, so you know everything! ", said Socrates. The self-recognition is the first step in the process of freeing yourself. Maybe you ask yourself: Do I really want that? Do I really want to pay this price? I dare you to ask a different question: Do I really want to continue paying the price of ambiguity within myself as well as difficult and unclear relationships in my life? Of course, It is your decision what you want for yourself. However, I would like to invite you to follow me through this book, diving into various topics and work yourself through the questions of self-knowledge. The reward for your personal effort will be invaluable and has the potential to change and transform your life profoundly in a positive manner. I call this method "Personality Enlightment" as you gain clarity about yourself while having the opportunity to experience some moments of enlightenment.

DiaMind-Questions:

1. In which area of my life am I not totally honest with myself and why do I not stick to my truth?

2. Why do I dread the clarity in this area?

2. Projections

A lot of problems and challenges in interpersonal relationships are based on projections. These projections are mainly negative and are accompanied with expectations. They have the potential to influence every relationship in a difficult and unfree way. You might ask yourself: "What are projections?" Projections according to Sigmund Freud, an Austrian neurologist and the founder of psychoanalysis, are a defense mechanism in which, for example, feelings and characteristics are transferred to another person. These ascriptions are not necessarily part of that person at all even if attributed from the outside. And yet, we tend to assume certain character traits. In a positive sense, this happens when we fall in love. We might assume a person is kind, interesting and intelligent. In a negative way, we project bad attributes towards people and claim that this person *is* like that. For example, the grumpy looking colleague, who seems unfriendly, boring and stuffy to us. Is this not crazy? By directing our projections at someone, we put them in a certain pigeonhole, from which they can only free themselves with difficulty convincing us of the opposite. Our negative projections are not just obstructive but they are able to reveal a lot about ourselves, our needs, our wishes and our imprints from our childhood. And finally: All negative projections can be helpful references about our unloved personality traits. Once we discover these and acknowledge them, we have the opportunity to change and transform them. Following the slogan:

"What you see is always a reflection of yourself in the mirror."

DiaMind-Questions:

1. Which **negative** attributes do I tend to see in others?

2. Which **positive** attributes do I often see in others?

3. Emotional Injuries

"If you don't heal your wounds, you will bleed on people who didn't cause them." (the saying is attributed to the German Sociologist Benjamin Painter). This slogan summarizes the deep impact that your unconscious mental wounds might have on others if not recognized, treated and healed. This ‚collateral damage' is likely to happen especially within close relationships like those to your own children or your partner.

I think it is important to recognize and accept the emotional injuries we received in our childhood and during our continuing life. Otherwise, they will influence our life and our relationships in an undesired and unclear way. Our wounds only hold control over us if we are unaware of them. Here, again, the potential and value of self-knowledge becomes clear and has the power to support you in your process of transformation. In German wound (Wunde) and wonder (Wunder) are orthographically connected, which begs the question if there is a deeper connection between the two. Maybe, they also belong together concerning their meaning as healing an emotional wound might feel like a wonder, would you not agree?

DiaMind-Questions:

1. I invite you to close your eyes:

→ Which key situations from my life come to my mind?

2. In which way do they affect my relationships today?

4. Deidentification – Releasing The Fixation

As human beings, we tend to identify ourselves with things and people in our lives. To be identified with something or somebody means, that something or somebody is experienced and viewed as inseparable, as belonging to us. This tendency leads to the conviction, that to a certain extent these things or people *are* a part of us. On the whole, it is fine to be identified with something or someone, yet it often correlates with entanglement and a lack of clarity. This would not be the case if we did not feel – and therefore: *be* – identified. Furthermore, the identification creates a fixation, a concentration on these things. This fixation refocuses our mind over and over again, and thereby aligns us towards something. The function of fixation at WhatsApp exemplifies this process. By fixating on particular chats, those find their way into your consciousness initially and your mind gets aligned with them. If these things or people contribute to your well-being, that is fine (also see positive projections). Yet, in many cases, the fixations are negative and contain similar impacts as described above in the chapter about "projections": We think that people or things *are* the way we perceive them. This is our subjective perspective, which does not necessarily coincide with reality - if there is one.

The good news: We have the power to become conscious about our identifications and fixations. The knowledge and clearance gained provide the first step in being able to *choose* new fixations or identifications- *or* not to choose them anymore and to release them from your life!

DiaMind-Questions:

1. What are the things and people in my life, with whomI am identified? Do those contribute to my wellbeing?

2. On which things is my mind fixed? On positive things and people or rather on negative ones?

5. Programming, Imprints And Beliefs

What is programming? Programmings are acquired/learned programs, which through countless repetitions turn into automatisms. As a neutral example, think of your morning routine of brushing your teeth. Mostly, this is programmed into our behavior during our early childhood. The positive effect of programs is that we do not need any mental energy for deciding whether to do something or not: we do it automatically. The example of teeth brushing shows the positive potential of programs as it is quite helpful not to start our days with discussing this with ourselves 😊 Yet, looking at other programs this is different. Maybe our parents were comforting us with chocolate when we hurt ourselves as small children. Now as adults, if we are facing stress at work or we feel hurt by our partner, this old program takes over and, automatically, we eat some chocolate hoping it will make us feel better (more about this topic in the chapter "Emotional Eating"). By recognizing our old programs, we have the chance to erase these and to replace them with new ones, more fitting and healthier programs (see Enlightening books for deeper understanding: Dr. Joe Dispenza).

Maybe you have already encountered the term "belief ". Beliefs are propositions whose content of truth is believed by us, and, hereby *become truths for us*. Unscrutinized and unconscious, those often negative dogmas have the power to hold us back within a reality similarly to sand bags in a hot-air balloon. Acknowledging these, I suddenly have the power to decide, which of these propositions I believe in and take as truths for my life. In order to become conscious about which beliefs operate inside me, reflection and vigilant introspection is necessary. Often beliefs are wordings/formulas we were frequently exposed to during our childhood. These got imprinted into our way of thinking and feeling and are still present within our current life. The negative potential of these beliefs is that most of the time they were negative wordings/formulas like „I am not enough. " or „I am too fat". Internalized, these phrases keep us small. By not becoming conscious and aware of these beliefs, they continue to unfold their negative potential. By that, they keep the past (childhood) activated and turn it into present (adult life). Taking the scientific insights of Quantum Physics of Dr. Joe Dispenza as a basis (see Enlightening books for deeper understanding), we create *our* reality through our thoughts and feelings. Your *Personality* is creating your *Personal Reality* – for better or for worse. If our thoughts are framed negatively, for instance, like the mentioned beliefs, they evoke negative feelings. As the past turns into the present, the present will become our future. Especially in this context, the process of self-knowledge and becoming aware is a great gift and contains the potential for an empowered creation of the life you really want to experience. By recognizing and identifying my beliefs, I have the power to transform them consciously and replace them with coherent and harmonious beliefs. When I am successful, I have the power to decouple my present and my future from the past and to actively create and experience a more positive present and future.

DiaMind-Questions:

1. Have you ever listened consciously to what stories your inner speaker tells you throughout the entire day?

Yes:	No:

2. If not: I invite you to do this for a whole day, writing down all the believes and often heard phrases in order to become aware of them.

1.

2.

3.

4.

5.

6.

6. Childhood And Inner Child

What does our childhood have in common with our inner child? During our childhood and adolescence, we experience a time that shapes us for our entire life. There are a lot of 'first-times' and new experiences we gain during this section of our lives. In early childhood, for example, learning to talk and to walk are crucial milestones. As we are influenced by 'normal' adults – in most cases our parents – who care for us *in the way they are able to,* it is impossible to avoid negative experiences. All positive and, especially, all negative experiences are accumulated within us. Therefore, these experiences which are originally from the past, are likely to trigger the inner child and, thus, get reactivated within the adult-I and stay present. These processes in most cases continue until we consciously recognize and transform them. As described in chapter 3, the process of self-awareness of our programs and injuries from our childhood is crucial in being able to responsibly create healthy and fulfilling relationships in the present. Therefore, it is not necessary to repeatedly play the drama-game and have power struggles, which I will further explain in chapter 19.

DiaMind-Questions:

1. If I concentrate on my inner world: Which positive and which negative experiences rise to my consciousness?

Positive Experiences	Negative Experiences

2. Do I have relationships in my life, in which those experiences create a different feeling, thinking and acting than I would perceive from my adult-I?

7. Parents

Only few functions are linked to as many projections, expectations and high demands as parenthood. In the analysis of my own parents, their biography and my expectations what they (supposedly) have not given to me, what they *should have been given to me as good and loving parents*, I gained the following trivial, yet mind-blowing insight: **My parents could just nurture me with qualities they themselves had.** Basically, parents are just normal people, often with an injured inner child themselves, possibly with difficult or traumatic experiences, who tried to give everything they have. In general, this is what it looks like: *It was everything they had at the time and it was their best at the time.*

I plead for two things: Firstly, for a responsible and conscious development it is very helpful to release your parents from your demands and expectations, especially in respect to the responsibility for your own (mis)fortune. Instead, you could take on the responsibility for yourself as a grown-up person and, thus, make the best of your life in the present.

Secondly, I would like to speak frankly to the parents:

You do the best you *can*. You have done your best at every point. Like your children, you are – some more, some less – shaped by your emotional injuries and experiences. You are a very precious person, just like your children. I wish that you encounter your children in an equal, heartfelt manner eye-to-eye. I wish that you apologize to your children when you recognize some behavior or words from the (recent) past as mistakes. It is not important how long ago the mistakes lie, which caused emotional injuries in the soul of your children:

Through realization **and** acknowledgement, in my opinion, it is possible that the injury in the soul of your child as well as your dysfunctional relationship towards your child can be healed and transformed. This is a great opportunity for a new time together in the present and the groundbreaking of a happy and healthy relationship in the future!

DiaMind-Questions:

1. In which areas of my life do I refuse my responsibility and hold my parents accountable?

2. How could I possibly have hurt my children by belittling, insulting, patronizing (etc.) them? Did I apologize to them?

8. Promising and Forgiving – The End Of The 'Drama-Game'

Often parents and their children are greatly entangled by their respective biographies Their biographies are, in a way, intermingled and inextricably intertwined. Therefore, breaking off contact is a difficult undertaking, yet sometimes feels like the only 'solution' to break through the vicious circle of mutually hurting each other. This *can* be a legitimate step to allow yourself space and time for inner processes as well as reflections and, thus, being able to see your parents from a more distant and therefore clearer perspective. The approach just described is also transferable to other close and possibly dysfunctional relationships, for instance towards siblings or friends.

In this context, I would like to briefly discuss a part of the philosophy of Hannah Arendt, a German-American political thinker and philosopher, regarding *commitment* and *forgiveness*. Hannah Arendt described commitment as well as forgiveness as a conscious act by an individual competent to make decisions.

Forgiveness, on the one hand, is the conscious act of finding a way out of a never-ending circle of action-reaction-reaction... – and, thus, out of the vicious circle of drama and blame, e.g. the power struggles of blaming each other. Commitment, on the other hand, is to be understood here as a conscious act, as a pronounced declaration of a concrete intention that points to a new future.

Hannah Arendt pleads for not merely behaving, in the sense of an automated behavioral sequence, such as withdrawing money from an ATM. She rather advocates acting consciously, in choosing a suitable course of action responsibly and clearly from a multitude of available options.

I consider this approach to be very helpful in finding a way out of the valley of the drama game, as it is nearly impossible for either side involved to identify a behavior or an action as the first action. So, the eternal struggle to find the person responsible for the conflict can come to an end when one of the parties involved says "Stop!" or "I forgive you." Therefore, conscious acts break the vicious circle that has been going on up until now and ends it. Let it go, even if it was hurtful. For me, this is about letting go of what happened and not about an unfelt, positive reinterpretation of the injuries. This opens an opportunity for all those involved to act anew, to act directed into the future and not to reproduce the past over and over again (see also Chapter 5).

Briefly, I would like to introduce you to the Drama Triangle of Stephen Karpman, an American psychoanalyst:

The Drama Triangle is a social model of human interaction from the Transactional Analysis (you find great illustrations of the Drama Triangle on the Internet). When the Drama Triangle crossed my path for the first time, it blew my mind! Finally, I found an easy-to-use-concept of social roles and communications and gained a deep understanding what is *really* happening below the surface during interactions. Basically, there are three roles: the victim, the persecutor and the rescuer. Despite the use of all these roles every once in a while, every person tends to have a preferred role, which they often take. In this model, the victim is the strongest position. "Really?!", you may ask, "He is weak and needs help!" And there the rescuer within yourself shows up and feels encouraged to save the victim from the mean persecutor.

Long story short: The victim blames the persecutor for something. The persecutor feels the right to treat the victim like he does. And the rescuer feels the need to lead the (self-appointed) victim to safety. What happens here, is that *everyone* in this Triangle gives away his power to someone else: The victim gives his power to the persecutor by blaming. The persecutor gives his power to the rescuer by justifying himself. And the rescuer loses his power to the poor and seemingly helpless victim. What do you guess is the strongest role in this Triangle? You are right: The victim is in the strongest position as without one person taking on this role, the role of the blamed persecutor and the rescuer are obsolete.

All of these roles have disadvantages: First, the communication is asymmetrically up or down. Second, you are not taking on **your** responsibility. By avoiding your responsibility, you give your center away and lose power. I invite you to reflect on this model and gain clearance about your personal and business situations in which this Drama Triangle is at work.

There is a fourth position: The neutral position. Once you have decided to discover your part(s) in the Drama game, you are able to step out of the Triangle and self-aware consciously take care of your needs and values, without needing anyone to blame or be saved by.

"Why is this understanding so important?" you may ask. Without taking over **your** responsibility over your life, feelings and thoughts, you are victimizing yourself and you are not in the position to consciously create. So, this process of knowledge is about going from victim to creator of your own life!

DiaMind-Questions:

1. Am I ready to take responsibility for myself and not to let my actions happen passively controlled from the past or from other people's behavior in the present?

Yes:	No:

2. Which role do I tend to pick inside the Drama Triangle? In which contexts is it difficult for me to keep my center and stay outside of the Triangle, in the neutral position?

Space for reflection and own impulses regarding your past

45

Present

9. Consciousness - Or: To Be Aware

Maybe you are wondering what it is all about? This section is split into two complementary and slightly different zones. The consciousness is a kind of high awareness of things, people and life itself. For example, you can have a consciousness, a higher awareness of beauty in your life and be aware of it, perceive it as such and acknowledge it.

Consciousness on the other hand is a form of being present, of being in the here and now. I am not just somehow there and somehow live into the day, but I am aware of myself, my surroundings, the people in my life and my decisions, I am attentive and present and appreciate the value of people and things, my abilities and the possibilities in my life.

I do not passively let old programs and imprints determine my thoughts, feelings and actions but I actively choose the direction of what I perceive as reality for myself.

DiaMind-Questions:

1. How would I describe the awareness of my life? Through which glasses do I perceive my life?

2. Am I present and conscious and do I actively decide about the quality of my thoughts, my feelings and my actions?

10.   Inspiration

According to the Dictionary of Webster, inspiration means "an inspiring agent or influence; the action or power of moving the intellect or emotions". Part of the word inspiration is 'spirit', which is set in motion and ecstasy when we are in a state of being inspired. We can feel inspired by an interesting conversation, a film or even a newspaper article. When we feel inspired, we feel alive, wide awake and effortlessly present in the moment. We learn something new or discover something new within something old creating a different perspective. Sometimes it is text on postcards or a new place that we discover, and which inspires us and stimulates our spirit. What is inherent in all inspirations is the inner alertness and positive excitement that comes with one of the most vivid states of being. I, for example, experience this very intensely while writing and structuring this book and while talking to interesting people.

DiaMind-Questions:

1. Which people or things inspire me?

2. Do I represent an inspiration for my fellow human beings in conversations (i.e. Am I inwardly and outwardly present and awake and develop myself further and, therefore, the things I am talking about are always different)?

11.   Energy Follows Attention

What does this statement mean? It means that our energy, be it 'only' the mental one, goes where we direct our focus and attention (see Chapter 4). That which we direct our attention to becomes greater. For this reason, it is crucial to become aware of what you want to spend your energy on perceiving energy as a precious currency.

Two examples:

If I wish for a rich vegetable garden and go to sports in every spare minute and take short trips on the weekends, then it will remain a wish in the realm of ideas. If I really-really wish for a vegetable garden, it will mean dealing with the seasons, sowing and watering the seeds, tending and caring for them.

The other example is about close relationships, for example with your own children or your partner. By constantly criticizing and pointing out what bothers me and what is not right for me, I draw my attention to the negative area and the frustration becomes greater for me - but also for everyone else.

It is enough not to comment on the negative but we must educate and train ourselves – and our brain – to note only the pleasant things. In this way the disturbing can slowly disappear from perception and the positive grows and becomes bigger in perception. The vicious circle of negativity thus becomes a blessing spiral of positivity.

DiaMind-Questions:

1. What do I focus on in everyday life and in my life in general?

2. Are these the things I wish to experience more in my life? If not: What do I wish for to become bigger and more in my life?

12. Thought Movements

Some time ago I was at a Satsang. In Indian philosophy, a Satsang is a gathering of people who seek and strive for the highest truth by asking questions together, listening, thinking and reflecting. At this session an ambassador of wisdom spoke: "If a problem arises as a problem before you, then go back to love with your thoughts. It is a simple thought movement. In love, in unity, there are no problems. There are only things that are as they are, with all their inherent potential. As soon as you realize that something is perceived as a problem by you, go back to oneness."

The ego creates the separation of I and you, of love and problem in our polar world, but in the essence, everything is one. We are able and, in a position, to remove the separation and restore the oneness through a conscious thought movement. Both, the possibility and ability of consciously deciding which thought to follow, have the power to give you the valuable experience of being the creator of your experience – instead of being the match ball of your thoughts.

DiaMind-Questions:

1. In which area or areas of life do I often experience problems (the feeling of being separated)?

2. What benefit do I have from this?

13.   Responsibility

The subject of responsibility is a common theme throughout this book. But what exactly does responsibility mean? According to the German dictionary Duden, responsibility is a "[duty associated with a certain task, a certain position] to ensure that (within a certain framework) everything takes the best possible course, that what is necessary and right is done and that no harm is done." The definition may sound a bit unwieldy at first glance but it can help to gain clarity about different areas of responsibility and thus help us become aware of our own responsibility.

In concrete terms: What can I do or not do in this situation to achieve the best possible result? What could be my contribution to the success of a process? What factors are my own that could thwart a good result and how can I change my attitude and behavior to meet my responsibilities? This is also about the evolution from victim to creator of your own life (as you experience it). For although we do not bear the responsibility for our growing up and the negative experiences associated with it, we do have the responsibility - and thus also the positive power - to shape our present and future positively for ourselves.

DiaMind-Questions:

1. What do I acknowledge as my areas of responsibility?

2. In which areas of life do I reject to accept my   responsibility?

14.　Decisions And Intuition

As an introduction to this book, we have familiarized ourselves with the value of self-knowledge in the first chapter. In contrast to self-knowledge, which is based on reflection and a conscious cognitive process, intuition is a rather sudden realization that becomes conscious and is based on a safe feeling. In a way, we can equate self-knowledge with the head and intuition with the heart or gut feeling. To be able to make really sustainable, good decisions for ourselves and our lives, it makes sense to base decisions on both reflected thoughts as well as intuition. It is important that we take the time to order and weigh arguments consciously (as) objectively (as possible) However, it is also important to eventually get to the point where we make a decision. If we do not ever decide, life often takes over for us - with all the often negative consequences. I would like to encourage you explicitly to make mistakes as well as to risk wrong decisions! This is part of human life and (almost) every decision can be corrected if necessary. To say it with Kant and his "Sapere aude!": "Have the courage to use your own mind" And I add: Listen to your intuition and connect both poles harmoniously as a basis for your decisions!

DiaMind-Questions:

1. How does my decision processes work?

2. In which areas of life do I find it difficult to make decisions? Why?

15.   Emotional Eating

This topic will probably not be of interest to everyone and I have thought long and hard about whether to approach it at all in this book. I have come to the conclusion that as it is a challenge for many people, it should not be missing here. If eating is not an emotional topic for you then please feel free to skip this chapter or read it in order to support a friend, for whom it can be useful as inspiration.

Most of us in the so-called first world (with a few exceptions) live in a world of abundance and plenty. This also applies to the availability of food. Just a few of us succeed in consuming exactly the right amount of healthy and growth-promoting food over the course of our lives. We often eat not only for the reason of food intake, but also out of habit, enjoyment, sociability and sometimes even frustration. This is where emotional eating comes into play, already briefly mentioned in chapter 5. By emotional eating I understand consumption of food without the body really being hungry.

One example: You come home after a long and exhausting day at work and you are exhausted. Everything in you craves relaxation and reward as compensation for the hard work you have done. You cannot exactly feel whether you are actually hungry; too many impressions and stimuli have been dripping down on you during the day. As if controlled remotely - in the truest sense of the word! - you go to the fridge and grab chocolate or pudding and let yourself fall onto the sofa. Unconsciously you consume the food, perhaps while the TV is on. At some point you think that you have not eaten anything proper and you cook something. It is not easy to cook the right amount for one person and so you finish your entire plate every evening as if there were no tomorrow.

At some point you wake up from this routine and look at your body as a logical result of your unconscious eating behavior and want to change something.

I invite you to ask yourself "Why?" before every food intake. Do I want to eat something now because I want to reward myself? Have I experienced (emotional) stress today and do I deserve a positive, delicious compensation? Do I feel anxiety or frustration and quickly want to stop feeling these feelings with the help of sugar? Do I unconsciously rebel with my eating behavior against my partner or a parent and perceive it as freedom to eat what I want, when I want and how much I want? Do I, my soul, my spirit and also my body, rather need relaxation or a soothing conversation with a friend? Or would a stimulating read and a hot bath actually be much more relaxing? Or: **Am I actually physically hungry?**

Often our relationship to food and our eating habits stem from our childhood and have been programmed into us through formative experiences (see Chapter 5). Maybe our grandmother used to cook our favorite sweet dish for us and that dish is now much more than that to us: This special sweet dish represents for us unconditional love, warmth, a safe space, care, peace and quiet and being in a good mood. We actually consume all of this when we eat for example a warm vanilla pudding, and thus nourish our soul rather than our body.

However, mental and emotional hunger can never be satisfied with food.

DiaMind-Questions:

1. Which dishes have a deeper emotional meaning for me than simple food intake for my body? What do I associate with these foods?

Food/ dish, feelings and meaning for me:

1.

2.

3.

4.

2. What could I do instead of eating when I long for relaxation, the feeling of closeness or love?

*

*

*

*

*

16. Alone or: All-One

Being alone is often equated with loneliness in public perception and inner experience. I would like to clearly distinguish these two terms and explain their difference. While loneliness refers to social isolation, being separated from our fellow human beings in daily life, being alone is something completely different.

When I am alone with myself, I am whole, complete, connected with everything inside of me. I have the opportunity to listen to the silence and wisdom within me, to develop a sense of my inner voice and the answers that come from my heart. Nothing distracts me from myself and my being in these moments. This can be wonderfully experienced through the immersion in meditation. In meditation I am completely with myself, close my eyes so that my inner world is more real than the outer world in which I live with my body. I feel connected with the whole, the universe, everything, and I draw strength, silence and joy that I can share with my fellow human beings in due course. Thoughts clear up, new truths and insights rise in my consciousness and I feel whole, all-one. This is the hidden potential that lies in being alone and what each and every one is capable of unfolding and developing positively for their own life.

DiaMind-Questions:

1. How do I experience myself when I am alone?

2. Do I already have experience with meditation? Which one?

17. The World And Me

After focusing on the importance of being alone in the previous chapter, I would like to devote this chapter to meaningful and necessary additions: My being and my success in the world. In the present, it is always important to take stock of personal milestones and successes. Why, you might ask yourself? Sitting down and reflecting on the successes you have already achieved in your life and the positive things you have brought into the world can give you courage, strength, confidence and self-worth. It enables you to become aware of your potential already unfolded and encourages you to think about concrete steps on how you want to actively shape your life in the future. It is important to not only focus on yourself but also on the good you have created and can create for other people and the world.

An example to illustrate this: Anna is in her late 40s, sitting in her study and reflecting on her personal achievements. The first things that come to her mind are her high school diploma, her completed studies and her very successful career. These are, so to speak, the 'hard facts' of her measurable external success. Anna continues to reflect. After all, her life is not simply her professional career. That is only one aspect of it. So, she continues thinking about her achievements and more and more things, which she feels are successes, come to her mind:

- Her two children, whom she raised alone and lovingly

- her father, whom she accompanied attentively and with dignity on his last journey

- the single, neighbor with depression who, through Anna and her children, experiences family connection and thus warmth and safety within a community

- the student, she supports as a mentor on their personal and professional path

- the association she founded to promote an awareness of the connection between humans and nature

- her sponsorship of an Indian girl with limited educational opportunities

- her kind and appreciative words for the garbage collectors, which bring a smile to their faces and give them joy

- a fulfilling, mindful partnership, which nourishes and allow both her and her partner to grow in a wonderful way

- …

As you can see from the long list of inspiring things, unfolding your potential involves more than just what is important and right for you personally. Rather, it is about placing yourself in an all-encompassing, interconnected web of a local and global world. So, you can make your mark in a light-filled and profitable, sustainable and dedicated way in the service to other people and nature. The Spanish word for 'serve' is 'ser vir'. Literally it means 'being alive' and it is, because if you unfold your potential in serving the world and all beings, you will feel infinitely alive and inspired. How do you want to make a positive difference in the lives of others and contribute to the evolution of the world?

DiaMind-Questions:

1. What are the measurable achievements of my life so far?

1. Achievement	
2. Achievement	
3. Achievement	
4. Achievement	
5. Achievement	

2a. What are the other successes of my life with which I have brought my light into the world?

1. Achievement	
2. Achievement	
3. Achievement	
4. Achievement	
5. Achievement	
6. Achievement	
7. Achievement	

2b. What are the future achievements that I would like to bring to the world, to serve the world and thereby (also) myself and to enrich it with my evolutionary footprint?

1. Achievement	
2. Achievement	
3. Achievement	
4. Achievement	
5. Achievement	
6. Achievement	

Space for reflection and own impulses to the present

Future

18. Who Am I And Who Do I Want To Be?

Do you know who you are? Do you have any idea who you could be? Dealing with these questions could lead you to the realization that you are not a stringent individual personality, but rather a patchwork personality - you are not always thinking, feeling and acting in the same way but rather differently By being different and living out different qualities and behaviors, you could come to the conclusion: "Yes! That's me! And that! And that and that too! WOW!" This insight gives you freedom. The freedom to bring your whole multifaceted being into the world and to express it.

How is the image of your personality created? You create it by repeating the story of your life, your experiences, and most importantly by evaluating your imprint in your mind over and over again. These thoughts about yourself and your past create thoughts and feelings in the present and thereby create the perspective and experience of your future. This might not be good news for you at first. Because by repeating your bad and negative experiences again and again, you reinforce them as identical with your Self and keep yourself in the past. Why? Very simple: Energy follows your attention, the aspect to which you direct your energy becomes bigger and identifications with the past tie you to it.

However, there are some good news: Charles R. Swindoll, a Protestant Christian pastor, author, educator and founder of *Insight for Living* stated: "I am convinced that life is 10% what happens to me and 90% how I react to it." Let us assume that a situation is made up of about 10% things as they are, and about 90% of your reactions, evaluations and interpretations thereof. That means that there is hidden treasure, an incredible potential that you can discover. You cannot change the situations and experiences of the past in the present. But you **can** change the remaining 90% in your consciousness at any time. This gives you the power to tell your story anew and emotionally create a different experience in your life. What an opportunity!

DiaMind-Questions:

1. Which story do I tell about myself and my past? Do I view it positively or negatively?

2. Do I want to continue telling this story or would it do me good to create a new story? How would this story about me and my life look like?

19. (R)Evolutionary Partnership – Love Instead Of Fear

(R)Evolutionary partnership? "What is that?", you may ask. What makes a partnership (r)evolutionary? Not so long ago, marriage served to raise children through a wife's service at home and a husband's economic provision for the family through gainful employment outside the home. Strictly speaking, it was not only the wife who depended on the husband's financial support. It was also the husband who depended on the wife, who looked after the children and the household in his absence. This has changed fundamentally: Today women often do just as much paid work as men, in fact they expect to be able to do just that. This, together with the significantly expanded range of day-care facilities for children, has, in part, created beneficial social conditions to further development of partnerships compared to the past. (R)Evolutionary partnerships are based on equality and voluntariness. A (r)evolutionary partnership as I understand it is based on freedom in many ways. Both partners remain independent personalities, who continue to develop and grow within themselves and with each other, not to forget also through each other. They live the principle of mutual freedom from expectations. Each partner is or becomes aware of his or her personal needs and takes full responsibility for their fulfilment. The fulfilment of needs and the 'production' of happiness is not imposed on the partner. Each partner gives to the other partner without expecting anything in return. Both partners respect the diversity and experience as inspiration rather than as a threat. (R)Evolutionary partners are, in the truest sense of the word, partners and partners along the path and life of the other. A fundamental mutual gratitude conveys appreciation to each partner and nourishes the souls and thus also the willingness to grow. Central in a (r)evolutionary partnership is also self-responsibility, which, among other things, is shown in the clearest possible, non-violent communication from the I-perspective. A (r)evolutionary partnership is lived in a growth-oriented and not a fear-oriented way. What does this actually mean?

I will explain this with an example: If you are afraid that your partner might find their friend more attractive than you, in a conventional partnership you might then agree that she will no longer meet him alone but only together with you. So, you would give your fear of loss priority over her freedom to meet with her friends. In a (r)evolutionary partnership you would look at your fears closely instead and try to discover from where they originate. Jealousy, for instance, often results from a deep fear of loss and a lack of self-esteem. You try to understand and resolve your fears rather than continuing to project them onto your partner's friend (see Chapter on projection and responsibility). This assumption of responsibility gives you and your girlfriend a great deal of freedom and brings about trust in yourself and in your relationship.

In this context I would also like to introduce the image of the 'drama pool'. You know a swimming pool that you can walk around, jump into and swim in. Suppose you say something to your partner that evokes feelings from their childhood and he figuratively falls into the drama pool. Perhaps by fighting you with words that are, in fact, meant for his mother (see also Chapter 3, Projections in proxy fights). He may behave like a raging little hurt child and may say or think something like "Now you're making me behave like an idiot again!" Remember the Drama Triangle and its implications! Now you have two options/ two ways to react.

Option 1: Either you let yourself fall and struggle with him in the drama pool, i.e. by defending yourself against his attacks. This way, you hurt each other with words and reproaches. Afterwards, you are exhausted and further apart than before.

Or you choose option 2: You are present and conscious enough in the moment and recognize the situation your partner is in. Calmly you stand at the edge of the pool and wait for him on the ladder until he has done enough laps in the drama pool and is ready and able to recognize that his drama is happening only inside of him and has nothing to do with you or your relationship. Now you can reach out to him and he can come out of his drama pool wet and shaken inside, yet an insight richer.

I love this image because it shows impressively how being present, self-knowledge and the assumption of personal responsibility in yourself and in a partnership, can influence outcomes positively. In order to avoid misunderstandings, it is important to me to point out that during this I am not leaving my partner abandoned if he has fallen into the pool. I am and always will be a loving counterpart to him. However, it is important at this point that the drama loop can be interrupted and that the partnership is not lived unconsciously and destructively. When emotional wounds are flushed out of your partner, it is important to stand by him and bear his pain with him - without transferring this pain into your partnership our onto yourself through projections.

Through focusing on growth when choosing one of the two options, the connection becomes clearer, deeper and more intimate despite increasing freedom. The whole partnership develops into an openness rather than ending sooner or later in a dead end - followed by either inner resignation or outer separation. This openness carries both partners into a common, fulfilled and open future. The entire (r)evolutionary partnership is summed up by:

"The I experiences itself at the You and recognizes itself in the We." (by Lea-Johanna Borkenstein)

DiaMind-Questions:

1. What are my needs in general and in a loving relationship?

For Myself:	In a loving relationship
1.	1.
2.	2.
3.	3..
4.	4.
5.	5.
6.	6.
7.	7.

2. Which themes and drama situations are repeated in my partnership? How did I react and how do I want to react in the future instead?

Situation	Old Reaction	New Action

20. Potential Evolvement

In Chapters 17 and 18 we have briefly touched on your personality. Now we will go one step further and think about your potential. What does potential mean? It is the talents and abilities that are already present in you as a possibility, even if you have not yet given them room to become visible and develop; maybe you have not even recognized them as such! These can be creative or technical, musical or agricultural skills. No matter which talents you recognize as your potential: Only when you find out what these talents are, can you unfold them and thus experience, live and bring many more facets of your personality into the world. Why is this important, you may ask? Maybe you have been working for many years in a job that does not match your Self, your values or your abilities. I think it is essential for a happy, fulfilled and healthy life that you discover your potential, develop your present life out of your inner 'padded cell' and lead a life that really suits you, both professionally and privately.

DiaMind-Questions:

1. What talents and abilities do I have, which I do not incorporate in my life yet?

2. I invite you to ask five or more people in your life what talents and abilities they see in you! You will be amazed!

21. My Vision - Or: Wishes Are Memories That Come From The Future

What do you dream about? What is your idea of an ideal, suitable, happy life for you?

What is your vision?

A vision is something you wish for and already see and feel inside of you. However, this has not yet become visible in the tangible world. To give you an example: A woman who wishes to have a child carries an inner intuition, an image of a baby that has not yet shown itself as a real baby in her reality.

My vision, for example, is the creation of a DiaMind-Center as a place for inner growth, for meeting, for learning and self-knowledge, for joy and for the development of potential, for (r)evolutionary partnerships and lived philosophy.

I invite you to close your eyes and let yourself slide completely into your inner world. What do you see? What do you feel? What does life look like that you see and that fills you completely and lets you be with yourself?

DiaMind-Questions:

1. What is my vision of a fulfilled life?

2. Which concrete steps can I take to make my vision come true?

1.	6.
2.	7.
3.	8.
4.	9.
5.	10.

22. Personal Growth - Or: Towards The Sun

Personality development means developing what is hidden inside you and realizing the potential that is inherent in you. It is about bringing light into darkness, recognizing your Self and growing. The same applies when we take a look at nature: **The only proof of life is growth.** Even trees do not stay underground with their roots but grow higher and higher towards the sun. Why can we humans want that, to develop and grow, despite all possible painful insights, you may ask? Because the air up there is much better and we can breathe and live much more freely there, without fear, narrowness and darkness.

Some time ago I came across a 'translation' of the English word 'fear' into an acronym. 'Fear' stood for 'Face everything and rise'. I think that is beautiful and very appropriate because as soon as we look things in the face and recognize them and stop running away from them and suppressing them, they lose their power over us. What a gift that we can give ourselves at any time! When we give up old fears that have long since ceased to suit us, we also give up a part of our personality, our previous identity. This first creates on one side relief and perhaps for a short time on the other side also a vacuum and thus uncertainty. In your further development, however, this opens up a free space, which you can use in favor of a new personality, new feelings, new behavior and new decisions - and for the unfolding of your vision!

Another point is important to me in connection with inner growth. It touches on the questioning of possible addictive behavior, which might play a role in your life. I am speaking here explicitly of addictive behavior and not of the recognized Addiction Disease, in order to clearly distinguish these at times overlapping and yet different concepts from each other.

I have observed that many people display behaviors and habits that go beyond what is healthy. For many people, this could be the consumption of sugar or food in general. For others, it is television or the unconscious use of other media such as computers and mobile phones. Still others very often indulge in alcohol, cigarettes and sex or work excessively. Whatever it is: an addictive use of the above or other things often serves to avoid confrontation with our own inner emptiness as well as trying to compensate for it. As already described in the chapter on Emotional Food, the soul actually longs for something else, for spiritual nourishment like human warmth, love, recognition, appreciation and exchange of ideas. These things are not always immediately available, often associated with effort and the fear of rejection. So, it is human and understandable to prefer other, more readily available things as compensation. Nevertheless, it remains exactly that: **a substitute that will never be able to nourish your soul.** You can only experience human warmth through other people and dealing with other people always carries the risk of rejection. However, inner growth and self-knowledge are worthwhile and can give you a new life!

DiaMind-Questions:

1. Is there something in my life that I am afraid of, but which I now want to face courageously?

2. Is there something in my life where I recognize addictive behavior? Do I know what I am actually looking for?

23. Last But Not Least: Everything Is A Process!

You did it! Congratulations! You have worked your way through the whole book, studied 22 topics and answered 44 questions about yourself! What a success! As you experienced yourself, the path to your truth leads through different layers of your being or: "The only way out is through."

I hope that you were able to enjoy your process in spite of effort and perhaps also unpleasant, even painful insights and that you came closer to yourself. I hope that now you really feel like digging deeper, being inspired and living and deepening your life in all imaginable facets. I hope that you can now go your own way empowered, that you have found more clarity and more personal freedom and have gained internal security. And now to continue courageously and full of confidence towards your truth, which is always new.

I would be very happy about a message from you on how you experienced your journey, whether my book was a helpful guide through your inner world or something else you think is worth sharing. Maybe you also have a question for me?

Write your message to mail@praxis-freiSein.de.

I am very happy to hear from you!

Love from the bottom of my heart,

Lea-Johanna

Space for reflection and own impulses for the future

24. My personal insights of the mindful journey to my essence

Enlightening Reading For Further Study:

A

- Arendt, Hannah: Vita active. 1967.

B

- Bambaren, Sergio: Die beste Zeit ist jetzt. 2012.
- Bucay, Jorge:
  1. Ich will ...: Das kleine Buch über die Liebe. 2017.
  2. With Bucay, Demián: Of Parents and Children: Tools for Nurturing a Lifelong Relationship. 2019.
  3. With Harrach, Stephanie: Drei Fragen: Wer bin ich? Wohin gehe ich? Und mit wem? 2013.
  4. With Salina, Silvia: Liebe mit offenen Augen. 2010.
  5. The Power of Self-Dependence: Allowing Yourself to Live Life on Your Own Terms. 2003.

C

- Chopra, Deeprak: The Seven Spiritual Laws of Success. 1994.

D

- Dispenza, Dr. Joe: Breaking The Habit of Being Yourself: How to Lose Your Mind and Create a New One. 2013.
- Dyer, Wayne W.: Your Erroneous Zones. 2001.

F

- Fromm, Erich: 1. To Have or to Be. 2013
  2. Escape from Freedom. 1994.

3. The Art of Loving. Harper. 2006.

G

- Gawain, Shakti: Creative Visualization: Use the Power of Your Imagination to Create What You Want in Your Life. 2016.

- Golas, Thaddeusz: The Lazy Man's Guide to Enlightenment. 1980.

- Gibran, Khalil: The Prophet. 1923.

L

- Lakhiani, Vishen: The Buddha and the Baddass. 2020.
- Lindau Veit: Soul on Fire. True Life Manifesto: Wake up and live your full potential. 2012.

M

- Mill, John Stuart: On Liberty, 1978.

O

- OSHO:
    1. Freedom: The Courage to Be Yourself. 2000.
    2. Love, Freedom, Aloneness: The Koan of Relationships. 2002.
    3. Emotions: Freedom from Anger, Jealousy & Fear. 2010
    4. Tantra: The Supreme Understanding. 2009.

R

- Riemann, Fritz: Anxiety: Using Depth Psychology to Find a Balance in Your Life. 2009.

- Roach, Geshe Michael:

1. The Diamond Cutter: The Buddha on Managing Your Business and Your Life, 2009

2. Karmic Management: What Goes Around Comes Around In Your Business and Your Life. 2009.

- Rosenberg, Marshall B: Nonviolent Communication: A Language of Life, 3rd Edition: Life-Changing Tools for Healthy Relationships. 2015.

S

- Spenst, Dominik: 6-Minutes-Diary. 2019.
- Spezzano, Chuck:

1. Das Buch der Erkenntnis. 2010.

2. If It Hurts, It Isn't Love: And 365 Other Principles to Heal and Transform Your Relationships. 2000.

T

- Tolle, Eckardt: The Power of Now: (20th Anniversary Edition): A Guide to Spiritual Enlightenment, 2020.

V

- Valenteano, Ralph: Das Lächeln der Liebe – Der siebenstufige Pfad zu einer erleuchteten Beziehung. 2011.

W

- Winter, Andreas: Abnehmen ist leichter als zunehmen. 2017.

Z

Zurhorst, Eva-Maria:

1. Love Yourself, and it Doesn't Matter Who You Marry. 2007.

2. Liebe Dich selbst und entdecke, was Dich stark macht. 2012.

Appreciation and thanks

I would like to take this opportunity to express my deep gratitude to all those who have contributed and are contributing to my life. I thank each and every one of you for the change of perspective, development potential, joy, love and courage. I thank the inner and outer world for all the possibilities of insight and transformation, growth challenges and learning fields. I am deeply grateful for the experience that in every situation there is a bright, shining diamond hidden, just waiting to be uncovered.

Especially deep thanks are due to my children and my life companion - these people are my greatest development accelerators and source of profound happiness!

www.ingramcontent.com/pod-product-compliance
Lightning Source LLC
Chambersburg PA
CBHW051211250726
48655CB00006B/2355